SPORTS SUPERSTARS

PATRICK MAHOMES

By Kevin Frederickson

Kaleidoscope
Minneapolis, MN

Your Front Row Seat to the Games

This edition is co-published by agreement between Kaleidoscope and World Book, Inc.

Kaleidoscope Publishing, Inc.
6012 Blue Circle Drive
Minnetonka, MN 55343 U.S.A.

World Book, Inc.
180 North LaSalle St., Suite 900
Chicago IL 60601 U.S.A.

Kaleidoscope ISBNs
978-1-64519-045-5 (library bound)
978-1-64494-202-4 (paperback)
978-1-64519-146-9 (ebook)

World Book ISBN
978-0-7166-4349-4 (library bound)

Library of Congress Control Number
2019940064

Printed in the United States of America.

TABLE OF CONTENTS

CHAPTER 1

A Left-Handed Miracle

Quarterback Patrick Mahomes looks at the defense. He yells out to his Kansas City Chiefs teammates. The Denver Broncos fans cheer loudly for their team.

It's a **fierce** game. The Chiefs are losing. Time is running out. But Mahomes is moving his team down the field. He knows a touchdown would give them the lead.

Mahomes gets the ball. His wide receivers race down the field. His linemen push the defenders away. Moving around, Mahomes stares downfield. No one is open. The crowd cheers louder. The young quarterback **scrambles**. This buys more time. But he feels the defenders getting close.

Patrick Mahomes directs his teammates before taking the snap against the Denver Broncos.

Mahomes usually throws with his right hand. This time he can't. A defender dives at Mahomes. His body is in an odd position. So he moves the ball to his left hand. Just before being tackled, he throws it. Teammate Tyreek Hill is waiting. Wide open, he brings the ball in. Then he cuts upfield. First down!

FUN FACT

Mahomes became the first quarterback to throw for 13 touchdowns in the first three games of a season.

Broncos defenders kept the pressure on Mahomes all game.

Chiefs fans were used to big plays from Mahomes. The 2018 season was a breakout year. This was only his fifth game as a starter. He had already shown he could throw the ball far. He could also throw it on target. Against Denver, he showed more. Mahomes could even pass with his left hand. His key play kept the Chiefs alive. Soon they scored a touchdown. They went on to win 27–23. That improved their record to 4–0.

Chiefs fans were thrilled. Their young quarterback was already a star. He would lead the team to 12 wins that season. And he'd have many more big plays along the way.

NO LOOKING

Baltimore Ravens defenders were closing in on Mahomes. He needed to get rid of the ball fast. To his right, Mahomes saw a receiver. The Ravens followed Mahomes's eyes. But the quarterback threw to his left. The no-look pass paid off. A receiver caught the ball for a first down. It was another amazing play for Mahomes in 2018. And this one helped the Chiefs win 27–24.

Mahomes was all smiles after he and the Chiefs beat the Broncos in Denver.

CHAPTER 2

Son of a Pro

It's a warm summer day. The sun is shining. No fans have arrived at the stadium yet. So Patrick Mahomes grabs a ball and jogs out onto the field. There are no football lines, though. This is a baseball diamond. Five-year-old Patrick is in New York. He begins playing catch at Shea Stadium, home of the New York Mets.

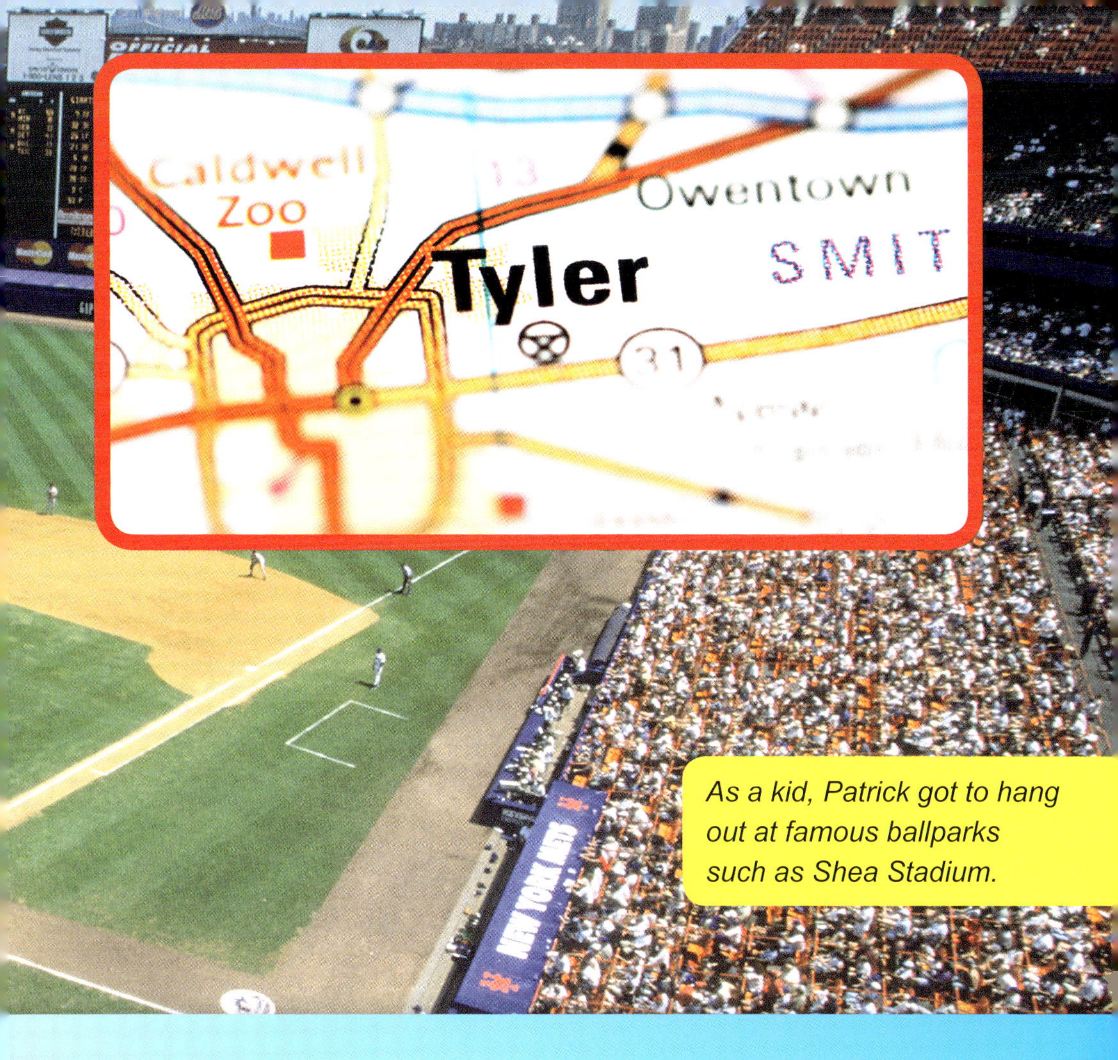

As a kid, Patrick got to hang out at famous ballparks such as Shea Stadium.

Patrick was born September 17, 1995. He was born in Tyler, Texas. He'd later go to school there. But he spent much of his childhood in different cities. That's because his dad, Pat Mahomes, played pro baseball. He was a pitcher. The family followed him. For a while, Pat played for the Mets. In 2000, the Mets even made the World Series.

Patrick learned a lot. He spent time in the **clubhouse**. His dad introduced him to star players. They talked to Patrick. He learned all about being a pro athlete.

A few years later, Patrick steps onto another field. This time it's a football field. He adjusts his brown jersey. Thousands of fans cheer. Patrick is a quarterback. He stars for his high school team in Texas.

Young Patrick got a chance to practice with his dad's teammates before a 2000 World Series game.

CAREER TIMELINE

1995

September 17, 1995
Patrick Mahomes is born in Tyler, Texas.

2014

November 1, 2014
Mahomes starts his first game as a college quarterback for Texas Tech University.

2016

October 22, 2016
Mahomes ties the college record for most passing yards in a game with 734.

2016

December 1, 2016
Mahomes wins the Sammy Baugh Award as the best quarterback in college football.

2017

April 27, 2017
Mahomes is selected in the first round of the NFL Draft by the Kansas City Chiefs.

2017

December 31, 2017
Mahomes makes his first NFL start. The Chiefs beat the Denver Broncos 27–24.

2018

September 9, 2018
Kansas City beats the Los Angeles Chargers 38–28. Mahomes is now the top quarterback for the Chiefs.

2018

December 30, 2018
Mahomes throws another touchdown pass, making him only the third quarterback ever to throw for 50 in a season.

2019

January 12, 2019
Mahomes wins his first playoff game, beating the Indianapolis Colts.

Three years later he steps onto a new field. This time his jersey is black. It's a big college football game. He plays for Texas Tech. The mighty Oklahoma Sooners are in town. Patrick is not scared. He takes the **snap**. His receivers run to the **end zone**. One gets open. Patrick swings his arm. The ball goes right to the receiver. Touchdown! The Red Raiders lost 66–59. But Patrick was great. He threw for 734 passing yards. That tied for the most in college football history. He also had five touchdowns.

Mahomes was ready for the next level. National Football League (NFL) teams agreed.

FUN FACT

Patrick also played baseball for Texas Tech as a freshman.

Patrick looks to pass during a college game.

With his great running ability, Patrick was hard to stop.

BASEBALL STAR

Patrick grips the ball. He moves it in his hand. Then he holds the ball tight. He kicks his leg and throws. Strike! In college, Patrick was also a star baseball player. He was a pitcher and outfielder at Texas Tech. Some thought he could go pro in that sport. But he quit after one season. It was time to focus on football.

CHAPTER 3

Standing Out

Patrick Mahomes pulls on his jersey. He adjusts his pads. Finally, his Kansas City Chiefs uniform looks just right. Then Mahomes grabs his shoes. One is red. The other is green. Each has a star. One shoe has "Team Luke" written on it. The other says "Hope For Minds."

These were special shoes. Mahomes wore them for one game. Team Luke is an organization. It helps kids who have had brain injuries. The shoes were sold after the game. The money went to Team Luke.

Mahomes does many things to help the **community**. One time, he surprised a youth football team. The players didn't know he was coming. They cheered when they saw him. Mahomes had gifts. He bought the entire team new helmets and jerseys.

Mahomes surprises local kids by buying them new football gear.

Where Mahomes Has Been

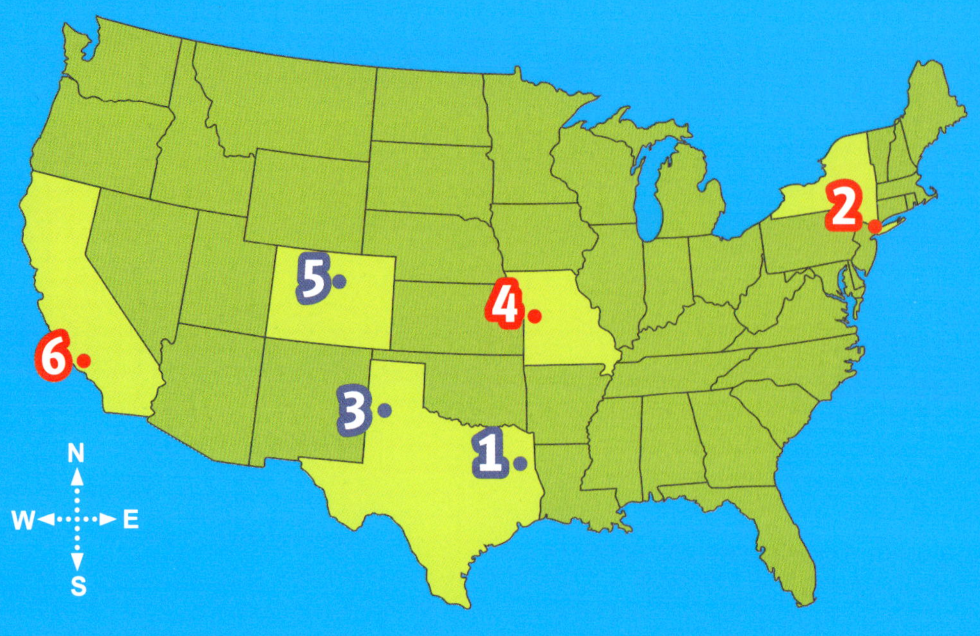

1 **Tyler, Texas:** Mahomes's hometown.

2 **New York, New York:** Mahomes spent time in different cities growing up, depending on where his dad was playing baseball at the time. Pat Mahomes played for the New York Mets in 1999 and 2000.

3 **Lubbock, Texas:** Home of Mahomes's college, Texas Tech University.

4 **Kansas City, Missouri:** Home of the Chiefs, Mahomes's NFL team.

5 **Denver, Colorado:** Mahomes made his first NFL start in 2017 on the road against the Broncos.

6 **Los Angeles, California:** Mahomes's first start in 2018 resulted in four touchdown passes and a win on the road against the Chargers.

Another time, Mahomes helped out in a different way. There was no practice that day. A military member needed a place to live. There was a house, but it needed work. So Mahomes grabbed a paintbrush. Soon he was painting a wall. His work helped make the house livable. Now the military member had a place to live.

Sports are important to Mahomes. He is also serious about education. In college he studied a lot. It paid off. Mahomes got good grades. He received awards for the good grades he got.

KETCHUP KING

Mahomes sits down for dinner. A bowl of macaroni and cheese is on the table. Mahomes grabs ketchup. He puts ketchup on everything. This grosses some people out. Mahomes doesn't care. He once got in front of a camera. He started putting ketchup on a bowl of macaroni and cheese. The video became a commercial for Hunt's Ketchup. Millions of people watched the ad.

CHAPTER 4

Chief of the Chiefs

Mahomes clapped his hands. He rocked back and forth. The young quarterback was ready to go. However, his first NFL start of 2018 would have to wait. The Chiefs were in Los Angeles. But the opposing Chargers had the ball. They punted. The Chiefs returned the kick for a touchdown. The wait continued.

Finally, it was Mahomes's time. He crouched low. The center snapped the ball. It pressed into Mahomes's palms. He threw it moments later. Wide receiver Tyreek Hill caught the pass up the middle. Defenders dove at Hill. They missed. Hill sprinted down the field. Touchdown! The Chiefs were on their way to a 38–28 win.

Mahomes lit up the Los Angeles Chargers in his first game as a full-time starter.

Playing on the road in Pittsburgh hardly slowed Mahomes down.

Mahomes was back a week later. This game was in Pittsburgh, Pennsylvania. Thousands of fans waved yellow towels. They were Pittsburgh Steelers fans. They wanted to see the Steelers beat Kansas City. Mahomes did not **panic**. He took the snap. He dropped back to pass. Then he whipped a pass. Wide receiver Chris Conley caught it in the end zone. Touchdown! After two weeks, the Chiefs had two wins. Mahomes had ten touchdowns.

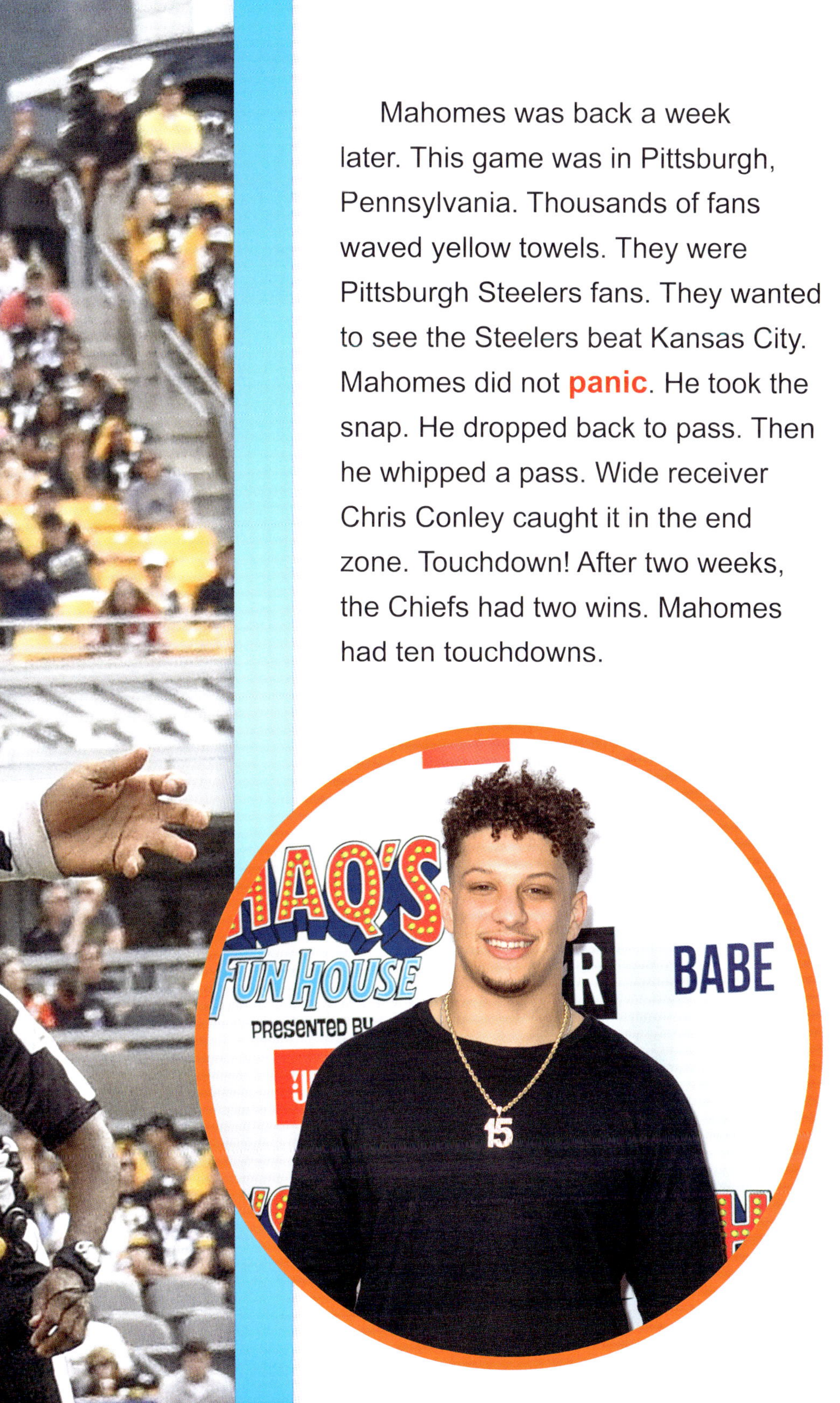

Through the 2018 season

PASSING YARDS	5,381
PASSING TOUCHDOWNS	50
COMPLETION PERCENTAGE	65.9
QUARTERBACK RATING	111.7

Mahomes directs his teammates from the line of scrimmage.

The touchdowns continued. Months later, the Chiefs were back home. A cold wind whipped through the stadium. The Chiefs were already headed to the playoffs. Now they led the Raiders 21–3. Mahomes didn't let up, though. It was the third quarter. Wide receiver Demarcus Robinson took off. Mahomes passed right to him. Soon Robinson was in the end zone. It was an 89-yard touchdown. That gave Mahomes 50 touchdown passes for the season.

The Chiefs were on a roll. At 12–4, they had the best record in the conference. It was playoff time. Mahomes and the offense were hot. They overpowered the Indianapolis Colts. Mahomes threw for 278 yards. He also ran for a touchdown.

Mahomes and the offense did their part in a 37–31 playoff loss to the Patriots.

The dream 2018 season ended one week later. The mighty New England Patriots came to town. Mahomes threw for four touchdowns. But the Patriots were too strong. The Chiefs fell in **overtime**. With Mahomes under center, however, the future looked bright.

BEYOND THE BOOK

After reading the book, it's time to think about what you learned. Try the following exercises to jumpstart your ideas.

THINK

THAT'S NEWS TO ME. In Chapter One, Mahomes makes a crazy left-handed throw. Learn more about that throw. Find an article online about that game. Read more about what happened before that throw. What were other important moments in the game?

CREATE

PRIMARY SOURCES. Primary sources are documents or sources that were made at the time of an event. They might include interviews, photos, and videos. Create a list of primary sources that talk about Mahomes. What kinds of information could you learn from these sources?

SHARE

SUM IT UP. Write a paragraph with the most important topics in this book. Use your own words. Do not copy from the book. Then share the paragraph with a classmate. What does your classmate think of your paragraph? Does he or she have any questions for you about Mahomes?

GROW

REAL-LIFE RESEARCH. What kind of place could you visit to learn more about football and Mahomes? What are some other things you could learn by visiting this place?

Visit www.ninjaresearcher.com/0455 to learn how to take your research skills and book report writing to the next level!

RESEARCH

SEARCH LIKE A PRO
Learn about how to use search engines to find useful websites.

FACT OR FAKE?
Discover how you can tell a trusted website from an untrustworthy resource.

TEXT DETECTIVE
Explore how to zero in on the information you need most.

SHOW YOUR WORK
Research responsibly—learn how to cite sources.

WRITE

GET TO THE POINT
Learn how to express your main ideas.

PLAN OF ATTACK
Learn prewriting exercises and create an outline.

DOWNLOADABLE REPORT FORMS

Further Resources

BOOKS

Frisch, Nate. *The Story of the Kansas City Chiefs*. Creative Education, 2014.

Lajiness, Katie. *Kansas City Chiefs*. Abdo Publishing, 2017.

Morey, Allan. *The Kansas City Chiefs Story*. Bellwether Media, 2016.

WEBSITES

Factsurfer.com gives you a safe, fun way to find more information.

1. Go to www.factsurfer.com.
2. Enter “Patrick Mahomes” into the search box and click 🔍.
3. Select your book cover to see a list of related websites.

Glossary

clubhouse: A clubhouse is where baseball players get ready for a game. Pat Mahomes hung out in the clubhouse before the game.

community: A community is a group of people who have something in common with each other. Patrick Mahomes helps people in his community.

end zone: The end zone is where someone has to go to score a touchdown. Mahomes runs into the end zone for a touchdown.

fierce: Something that is fierce involves a lot of intensity and aggression. The opposing team played fierce defense.

overtime: Overtime is an extra period of play if a football game remains tied after regulation. Despite their strong effort, the Chiefs fell to the Patriots in overtime.

panic: Panic means to be scared suddenly. Even when the Chiefs faced long odds, Mahomes stayed calm and did not panic.

scrambles: To scramble means the quarterback runs with the ball. When he can't find an open receiver, Mahomes often scrambles to try to gain yards on his own.

snap: The snap is when the center sends the ball to the quarterback to start a play. Mahomes took the snap and quickly threw for a first down.

Index

PHOTO CREDITS

The images in this book are reproduced through the courtesy of: Greg Trott/AP Images, front cover (center), front cover (right), 3; EFKS/Shutterstock Images, front cover (background top), front cover (background bottom); Margaret Bowles/AP Images, pp. 4–5; David Zalubowski/AP Images, pp. 6–7, 9; saje/iStockphoto, p. 7; Joseph Sohm/Shutterstock Images, pp. 10–11; sevenMaps7/Shutterstock Images, p. 11; Kathy Willens/AP Images, p. 12; Red Line Editorial, pp. 13, 18; Aspen Photo/Shutterstock Images, pp. 14, 15; John Sleezer/The Kansas City Star/AP Images, p. 17; Brent Hofacker/Shutterstock Images, p. 19; Jamie Lamor Thompson/Shutterstock Images, pp. 20, 23; Ben Liebenberg/AP Images, pp. 20–21; Don Wright/AP Images, pp. 22–23; Paul Jasienski/AP Images, p. 24; Ed Zurga/AP Images, p. 25; Jeff Roberson/AP Images, pp. 26–27; Mike Flippo/Shutterstock Images, p. 30.

ABOUT THE AUTHOR

Kevin Frederickson is a freelance writer and editor from Ohio. He lives near Cincinnati with his golden doodle, Max.